CRAFT BOX

ANCIENT ROMANS

12 projects to make and do

Published in 2014 by Wayland
Copyright © Wayland 2014

Wayland
338 Euston Road
London NW1 3BH

Wayland Australia
Level 17/207 Kent Street
Sydney, NSW 2000

Editor: Elizabeth Brent
Designer: Rocket Design (East Anglia) Ltd
Craft stylist: Annalees Lim
Photographer: Simon Pask, N1 Studios
Proofreader/indexer: Susie Brooks

The website addresses (URLs) listed in this book are correct at the time
of going to press. However, it is possible that contents or addresses may
have changed since the publication of this book. No responsibility for any
such changes can be accepted by either the author or the Publisher.

Picture acknowledgements:
All step-by-step craft photography: Simon Pask, N1 Studios; images
used throughout for creative graphics: Shutterstock.

A cataloguing record for this title is available at the British Library.
Dewey number: 937-dc23

ISBN: 978 0 7502 8394 6

10 9 8 7 6 5 4 3 2 1

First published in 2013 by Wayland

Printed in China

Wayland is a division of Hachette Children's Books,
an Hachette UK company.
www.hachette.co.uk

Contents

the Ancient Romans

The ancient Romans lived more than 2,000 years ago, ruling an empire that stretched from Britain through Europe to North Africa. Rome grew from a rich city ruled by kings into a republic, and then an empire.

The ancient Romans lived from about 750 BCE–480 CE.

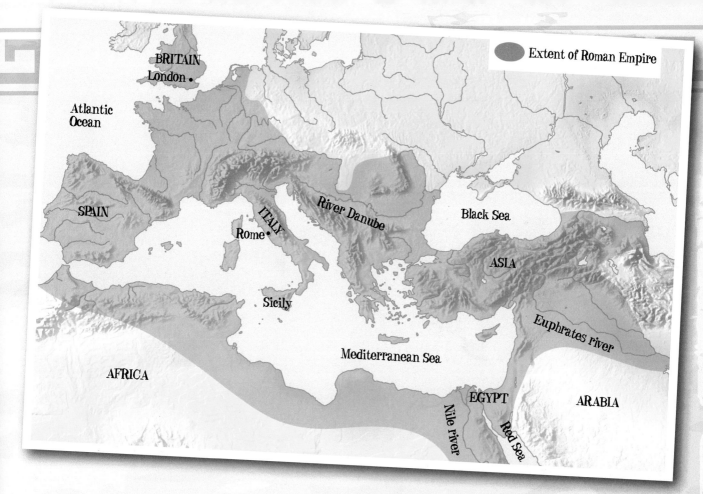

The map shows:
BRITAIN
London
Atlantic Ocean
SPAIN
ITALY
Rome
River Danube
Black Sea
ASIA
Sicily
Euphrates river
Mediterranean Sea
AFRICA
EGYPT
ARABIA
Nile river
Red Sea

Extent of Roman Empire

The ancient Romans were great architects and engineers. Roads and bridges linked cities and towns that boasted grand buildings, including games stadiums, temples, triumphal arches and private villas.

Many artists and craftsmen came to Rome from Greek colonies. They brought skills including sculpture, mosaic, glass, gem and metal work, fresco painting and pottery.

Some craftsmen worked in small workshops and learned their skill from a master, often their father. Others were slaves, who had been captured in foreign wars or born into slave families. They worked together in large workshops making dishes, pots and other objects. The materials they used, including stone, metals and gems, were traded across the Empire.

Roman remains, from buildings and mosaics to coins and clay lamps, can tell us lots of fascinating facts about life in ancient Rome. They can also inspire you to make some Roman crafts of your own!

make a
Roman shield

Roman soldiers fought with large shields that protected their whole body from their shoulders down to their knees. The shields were made from wood covered with leather, with an iron boss at the centre that protected the hand.

1 Cut the card into a rectangular shield shape.

2 Cover the card with red wrapping paper or foil. Fold back the edges and glue or tape them to the back of the card.

3 Cut strips of gold foil or card and fold them in half lengthways to cover the edges of your shield. Glue them in place.

Draw some eagle wings onto gold foil or card and cut them out. Cut thin arrow shapes from the foil or card. Glue the arrows and the wings in a symmetrical pattern onto the front of your shield.

Cut a circle of gold foil or card and glue it to the bottom of the tinfoil dish. Glue the dish to the centre of the shield.

Did you know...
Roman soldiers could lock their shields together like a defensive 'tortoise shell'.

6

Cut two strips of gold card to form handles, and glue or tape them to the back of your shield.

make a Janus mask

The month of January is named after the Roman god Janus. He is always shown with two faces, one looking to the future, the other one looking backwards to the Old Year.

You will need:
- Paper plate
- Paper
- Acrylic paints
- Brushes
- Marker pen
- Scissors
- Card
- Stapler

1 Draw around a paper plate onto a piece of paper. Sketch the design for your mask into the circle to make sure it will fit. If you need some ideas, look at pictures of Janus masks on the Internet or in books.

2 Draw a line down the middle of the paper plate and paint the two halves in contrasting colours.

3 Copy the outline of the mask onto the plate and cut it out.

4

Using your design as a guide, paint in the detail of the mask with acrylic paint.

5

Go round the details on the mask with a marker pen to make them stand out.

Did you know...
When Romans died, a wax mask of their face was carried or worn at their funeral.

6

Cut a strip of card and staple it to make a band that fits around your head. Staple the band to the top of the mask.

make a Dolphin mosaic

The Romans decorated the walls and floors of their houses and public buildings with mosaics. They showed colourful scenes of animals and birds, gods, goddesses and gladiators as well as geometric patterns.

1 Begin by deciding how big you want your mosaic to be, then use white paper to sketch out your dolphin. Look at Roman mosaics and photographs of dolphins in books or on the Internet for ideas.

2 Cut the coloured paper into strips about 2cm wide, then cut the strips into small squares and triangles to make mosaic tiles.

3 Stick rows of tiles that are all the same colour onto a piece of black paper or card, then draw the outline of a dolphin onto the tiles.

4

Cut the dolphin out.

5 Make your mosaic background by laying the tiles in rows onto another piece of black card. Mix up the colours to make a pattern, beginning at the outside edges and working in. When you are happy, glue the tiles in place.

Did you know...
Roman mosaics were made from thousands of small pieces of glass, stone or terracotta.

6 Stick the dolphin on top of the background mosaic.

make a
Roman coin box

The Romans minted coins made from gold, silver, bronze and copper. During the Empire, the coins showed the heads of the ruling emperor with an inscription in Latin and scenes of gods, myths, victories or battles on the tail side.

1 Cut down the cardboard packaging tube to stand about 6cm high. Leave a straight edge so the plastic lid will fit back onto the top.

2 Decide what your coin will show. Look at images of Roman coins in books and on the Internet to give you ideas. Draw around the lid of the tube, then sketch your idea into the circle you have drawn.

3 Draw around the lid onto the gold card and copy your design in the circle. Cut out the circle.

4

Glue the card circle onto the top of the plastic lid and allow to dry.

5

Cut a strip of card to cover the sides of the tube and stick it on.

Did you know...
A silver coin called a 'denarius' was a day's salary for a Roman soldier.

6

Use glitter glue to decorate the sides and lid of your coin box.

make a
Roman bulla

A bulla was a small pouch or locket worn around the neck by Roman boys and girls. Bullae were made of cloth, leather or gold and contained secret lucky charms or, sometimes, a magic word or spell.

1. Decide what will go inside your bulla. It could be anything from a lucky charm to a small coin or photo. Cut out two identical circles from the craft foam, big enough for your charm to fit inside, and a smaller square.

2. Cover the circles and the square with gold fabric and glue in place.

3. Place the charm inside one circle and then fit the other one over the top. Glue the edges of the circles together and hold them in place with clothes pegs while the glue dries.

4

Glue one edge of the square to the top of one side of the bulla. Place the middle of the cord in the square, then fold the craft foam over it and glue down. Hold it in place with a clothes peg while it dries.

5

Glue a piece of cord around the edge of the bulla.

Did you know...
A bulla was thought to protect children against bad spirits.

6

Decorate the bulla with glitter glue. If you want, you can tie the ends of the cord together so you can wear the bulla around your neck.

make a
Triumphal arch frame

The Romans built grand triumphal arches to celebrate their victories in battle. They were decorated with columns and carved stone panels and roundels showing battle scenes. Triumphant armies marched through them on victory parades.

1 Cut out an arch, a bit smaller than your photo, from one side of the box. Leave enough space above and below to decorate your arch. Look at triumphal arches in books and on the Internet to give you ideas.

2 Cut a cardboard tube a bit shorter than the arch, then cut it in half lengthways. Cut two circles from the card, one a bit smaller than the other but both bigger than the bottom of the tube, then cut them in half. Stick the smaller half circles to the larger half circles, then stick the tube halves to them. Cut the tinfoil dish in half and stick one half to the other end of each tube.

3 Stick the columns to either side of the box.

Cut two rectangles of card, wider and longer than the base of the arch. Stick one to the top of the box and one to the bottom.

Cut out strips and circles of card and stick them to the columns and to the front of the arch to decorate it.

Did you know...
Roman sculptors carved winged figures to represent victory.

6

Paint the arch with grey acrylic paint and leave it to dry. Then stick in a photo of your favourite sports team or star.

paint a
Roman fresco

The Romans decorated the walls of their houses and temples with paintings called frescoes. Sometimes they painted walls to look like marble or they painted false balconies and columns or windows. They also painted landscapes and scenes from Roman mythology.

1 Start by sketching out your ideas for your fresco. You could include birds or animals, or paint a person swimming or dancing. Look at pictures of Roman frescoes in books or on the Internet to give you ideas.

2 Take a piece of clay and work it with your hands to soften it. Then use the rolling pin to roll it into a flat tablet about 15cm by 20cm.

3 Use the clay tool to make holes in the top corners of the tablet so you can hang it up later.

4 While the clay is still damp, mix up a pale pink paint the colour of plaster and sponge it lightly over the tablet.

5 When it is dry, paint your design onto the tablet using the acrylic or watercolour paints mixed with water. You can use your fingers, the sponge and brushes to get different effects for your painting.

6 When the clay has dried, push the string or raffia through the holes to hang your fresco.

Did you know...
Fresco means 'fresh' in Italian. Fresco painting is done on wet plaster walls so the paint sinks in and the colours glow.

make a
Draco standard

A draco standard was carried by a horseman called a Draconarius in the Roman cavalry. It worked like a wind sock. Air passed through the dragon's mouth into its cloth tail so that as the horseman rode at speed, the standard made a hissing sound.

1 Paint the tube white and cut off one third.

2 Cut away a dragon's mouth shape at one end. Snip points around the mouth to make the dragon's teeth.

3 Cut a triangle with a wavy edge from the card to make a crest. Make a fold along the bottom edge of it and stick the crest to the dragon's head with masking tape.

4 Pierce a hole in the neck of the cardboard tube with the compasses and push the dowel through. Fix it in place with masking tape.

5 Paint the tube, crest and dowel gold.

6 Cut strips of crêpe paper about 50cm long and glue them to the dragon's neck. Cut a strip of crêpe paper about 12cm long and glue it inside the dragon's mouth to form a tongue. Draw a face on the dragon.

Did you know...

Draco standards were also used as targets in cavalry games. One team carried the standard and the other aimed javelins at the dragon's tail, scoring points for every strike.

make a
Laurel
wreath

The Romans wore wreaths made from laurel, the leaves of the bay tree, as symbols of rank and power. Roman emperors wore them as crowns. They were made in a horseshoe shape and sometimes decorated with ribbons and gems.

You will need:
- ▣ Large paper plate
- ▣ Scissors
- ▣ Pen or pencil
- ▣ Green construction paper
- ▣ Glue
- ▣ Gold ribbon
- ▣ Sticky tape

1 Cut the rim off the paper plate to make a base for your wreath. Then cut away a small section, snipping the ends into points.

2 Cut out leaf shapes from green paper. Look at pictures of bay leaves on the Internet or in books to help you. Cut plenty of leaves, both big and small, to make a full wreath.

Did you know... The Romans also made wreaths from oak and olive leaves, herbs and gold.

3

Fold the leaves and, beginning at one end, glue small leaves onto the base about a third of the way around, facing them towards the pointed end.

4

Glue some large leaves onto the middle third of the base, and finish with some smaller leaves at the other end.

5

Glue or tape a length of gold ribbon around the gap in the wreath to hold it in place. Wear the wreath with the ribbon at the front, you can tie more ribbons to the back to decorate it, too.

make a Roman seal

You will need:
- Pencil or pen and paper
- Mirror
- Air dry clay
- Blunt knife (non-serrated)
- Cocktail stick or clay tool
- Modelling clay

The Romans used seals made from gems, lead, bronze or clay to stamp and seal documents and parcels with wax. This was a way of making sure they were not opened while they were being carried by messengers.

1 Start by sketching out ideas for your seal. You could use one or two of your initials or a simple, symmetrical design. If you use your initials, you will need to carve them in reverse on your seal so use a mirror to help you.

2 Take a ball of clay and roll it with your fingers to form a cylinder shape. Cut each end of the clay to leave a flat surface.

3 Use a pencil to mark out your design or initials on one end of the seal. You can mark another design in the other end.

Use the cocktail stick or clay tool to carve the clay. You need to carve a small groove or V-shape along the lines in the clay.

Allow the clay to dry overnight. To seal an envelope, take a small stick of plasticene and flatten it into a disc. Press your seal into the modelling clay to leave your seal mark.

Did you know...
Roman craftsmen made bronze seal boxes to protect wax seals.

make a Roman clay lamp

The Romans lit their homes with clay oil lamps that could be held in the palm of the hand. Some were simple lamp shapes and some were made in the shape of a hand, foot, fish or other animal. The oil was carried by a linen wick to the spout.

You will need:
- ▣ Pen or pencil and paper
- ▣ Tea light or LED light
- ▣ Air dry clay
- ▣ Clay tools
- ▣ Rolling pin
- ▣ Glue

1

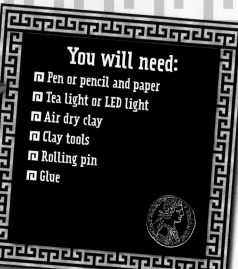

First decide on the design of your lamp. Look at the shapes of Roman clay lamps in books and on the Internet to give you ideas.

2

Use the tea light to guide the size of your lamp. It needs a small dish to sit inside. Take a ball of clay and work it with your hands to soften it.

3

Make a pinch bowl from the ball of clay, shaping a hole big enough for the tea light to sit inside. Make sure that the bottom of the lamp is flat so it stands safely.

4

Pinch the clay together at one end with your fingers to make a spout. Then pinch the clay together at the other end to form a simple handle.

5

You can use the clay tools to make decorative patterns in the clay. You could make straight or wavy lines around the hole and spout.

Did you know...
Lamp wicks were also made from papyrus and flax plants.

6

Make a lid by rolling out a piece of clay and cutting it to the same size and shape as the top of the lamp. Cut a circle, bigger than the tea light, and a smaller triangle from the lid, then glue it onto the top of the lamp. Allow the clay to dry and place your tea light or LED light inside.

make a
Roman sun dial

The Romans used sun dials to tell the time of day from the shadows cast by the sun. They had sun dials in public squares and on public buildings, and wealthy families sometimes had them in the courtyards of their houses.

1 Cut out a square and a triangle of strong card to form the base of your sun dial. The square will be the dial face, and the triangle will be the gnomon.

2 Use the craft knife or scissors and carefully cut out a slit in the centre of the square. Fold the triangle at the bottom and push it through the slit, with the right angle at the bottom. Glue or tape the folded edge onto the back of the dial.

3 Paint the dial face and the gnomon.

Use the marker pen and ruler to mark the dial face.

Add Roman numerals (see page 32) to the dial face.

Did you know...
Roman sun dials divided the day into twelve hours but they did not tell the time after dark.

⑥

Add a Latin motto. You can find lists of mottos on the Internet, such as Fruere Hora – Enjoy The Hour, or Tempus Fugit – Time Flies.

FRUERE HORA

FRUERE HORA

Glossary

Boss A round piece of wood or metal at the centre of a shield.

Bronze An orange-brown metal made from a mix of copper and tin.

Cavalry Soldiers who ride into battle on horseback.

Colony A country under the political rule of another country.

Empire A group of countries or people who have the same ruler.

Engineer Someone who designs and builds the working parts of engines, machines or buildings.

Flax A plant that the Romans used to make thread and then weave into fabric.

Fresco A wall painting on fresh, damp plaster.

Geometric Using mathematical shapes such as circles and triangles.

Gnomon The raised arm on a sun dial that casts the shadow that points to the hour.

Inscription Words printed, written or engraved on something.

Locket A necklace with a small case for containing a photograph or other memento.

Mint To produce coins.

Mosaic A picture on a wall, floor or ceiling, made up of small fragments of coloured pottery, stone or glass.

Mythology A collection of myths – ancient stories about gods, heroes and magical beasts.

Papyrus A plant that ancient civilizations used to make paper.

Republic A country, governed by people who are elected, that has no king or queen as head of state.

Roundel A decorative round panel or tablet.

Terracotta Brownish-red pottery or clay.

Wick A string running through a candle or a lamp that burns when it is lit.

Further information

BOOKS

Britain in Roman Times by Tim Locke (Franklin Watts, 2008)

Food and Cooking in Roman Times by Clive Gifford (Wayland, 2012)

The Gruesome Truth About the Romans by Jillian Powell (Wayland, 2010)

Hail! Ancient Romans by Philip Steele (Wayland, 2012)

History From Objects: the Romans by John Malam (Wayland, 2012)

Men, Women and Children in Ancient Rome by Jane Bingham (Wayland, 2009)

WEBSITES

http://www.bbc.co.uk/schools/primaryhistory/romans/
This BBC website is designed for Key Stage 2 learning.

http://library.thinkquest.org/CR0210200/ancient_rome/directions.htm
Packed full of information about Roman life, recipes and things to make.

http://www.britishmuseum.org/explore/cultures/europe/ancient_rome.aspx
Look at ancient Roman artefacts on the British Museum's website.

http://www.everyschool.co.uk/history-key-stage-2-romans-3.html
Lots of Key Stage 2 resources and information about ancient Rome.

Index

ROMAN NUMERALS

1 - $\overline{\text{I}}$ 6 - $\overline{\text{VI}}$

2 - $\overline{\text{II}}$ 7 - $\overline{\text{VII}}$

3 - $\overline{\text{III}}$ 8 - $\overline{\text{VIII}}$

4 - $\overline{\text{IV}}$ 9 - $\overline{\text{IX}}$

5 - $\overline{\text{V}}$ 10 - $\overline{\text{X}}$